# PAPER SOLDIERS OF NAPOLEONIC ERA -2

## PRUSSE & GERMAN ALLIED UNIFORMS FROM THE VINKHUIJZEN COLLECTION

SERIES EDITED BY

LUCA STEFANO CRISTINI

SOLDIERSHOP PUBLISHING
BOOK on DEMAND

## PAPER SOLDIERS SERIES

La collana è dedicata alla storia e alla collezione de mitici soldatini di carta o ai soldatini da wargame. In ogni volume preziose raccolte di soldatini stampati il secolo scorso (e anche prima), provenienti dalle nostre collezioni, ma anche nuovi figurini realizzati con abile maestria dai nostri bravi autori. Sempre con l'intento di fornirvi illustrazioni di grande qualità.

## RINGRAZIAMENTI E CREDITI FOTOGRAFICI - PHOTOGRAPHIC CREDITS:

Le tavole sono generalmente opera dell'autore o dell'illustratore indicato. La gran parte del resto dell'iconografia usata appartiene all'archivio dell'editore, foto scattate dall'autore, o materiale di amici collezionisti. L'Editore rimane in ogni caso a disposizione degli eventuali aventi diritto per tutte le fonti iconografiche dubbie o non identificate.

Title: **PAPER SOLDIERS OF NAPOLEONIC ERA - 2**
Serie edit by Luca S. Cristini. First edition by Soldiershop. December 2019
Cover & Art Design: Luca S. Cristini. ISBN code: 978-88-93275309
Published by Luca Cristini Editore, via Orio 35/4- 24050 Zanica (BG) ITALY. www.soldiershop.com

# PAPER SOLDIERS OF NAPOLEONIC ERA - 2

## PRUSSE & GERMAN ALLIED FROM THE VINKHUIJZEN COLLECTION

SERIES EDITED BY
LUCA STEFANO CRISTINI

# THE VINKHUIJZEN COLLECTION

This famous Collection of Military Costume Illustration consists of over 32,000 diverse pictures from varied sources of costumes mounted in 762 scrapbooks. Elaborate 19th-century European uniforms are the collection's special strength. The aesthetic quality of the images varies, as the collection includes 17th-century festival book prints, 19th-century chromolithographs, original watercolor compositions, pencil drawings, and photographs. Most are plates extracted from illustrated books and magazines.

all the pictures are organized by country and time period. The many scrapbooks devoted to Germany and Italy include separate designations for pre-unification states and principalities.

Assembled by one of these great, eccentric collectors of the late 19th Century, Dr. Hendrik Jacobus Vinkhuijzen, a Dutch medical doctor.

Dr. Vinkhuijzen traveled throughout Europe as a physician associated with various armies and with the Dutch royal court for. He began his career as a medical officer with the Royal Sharpshooters Corps in The Hague. During the Franco-Prussian War he served in France on an ambulance with the newly founded Red Cross. He also traveled to Russia, where he stayed in Moscow studying "the fight against pestilence." In his later life, he was the official court physician to Prince Alexander of the Netherlands. His father had performed in the same role for King Willem III.

ITALIAN TEXT

## LA COLLEZIONE VINKHUIJZEN

Collezionista eccentrico e appassionato cultore di iconografia militare era un contemporaneo del famoso uniformologo Quinto Cenni, visse infatti fra il 1840 e il 1910., il Dr. H. J. Vinkhuijzen, iniziò la sua carriera come medico dell'esercito olandese fino a diventare medico ufficiale di corte del principe Alessandro dei Paesi Bassi. La sua vasta collezione arrivò a contare oltre 32.000 soggetti. Moltissimi e pressoché sconosciuti fino alla loro pubblicazione nella nostra collana Quaderni Cenni, quelli realizzati espressamente per la sua collezione da parte del pittore emiliano. Dal 1911 la collezione è stata donata alla New York Public Library dal sig. Henry Draper erede del medico olandese. Ed è da questa collezione che Soldiershop prende i soggetti di questa nuova pubblicazione di soldatini di carta. Ogni immagine ha subito una rigorosa pulizia e ri-classificazione per fornire agli appassionati di storia militare e costume un'opera completa, agevole e utile per tutti gli studiosi e gli appassionati di uniformologia e non solo.

# THE PLATES
# OF PRUSSIAN ARMY

Prussia infantry 1806

Prussia infantry 1806

Prussia infantry 1806

Prussia grenadier 1806

Prussia grenadier 1806

Prussia grenadier 1806

Prussia horse dragoons 1806

Prussia horse dragoons 1806

Prussia horse dragoons 1806

Prussia hussars 1806

Prussia hussars 1806

Prussia hussars 1806

Prussia cuirassiers 1806

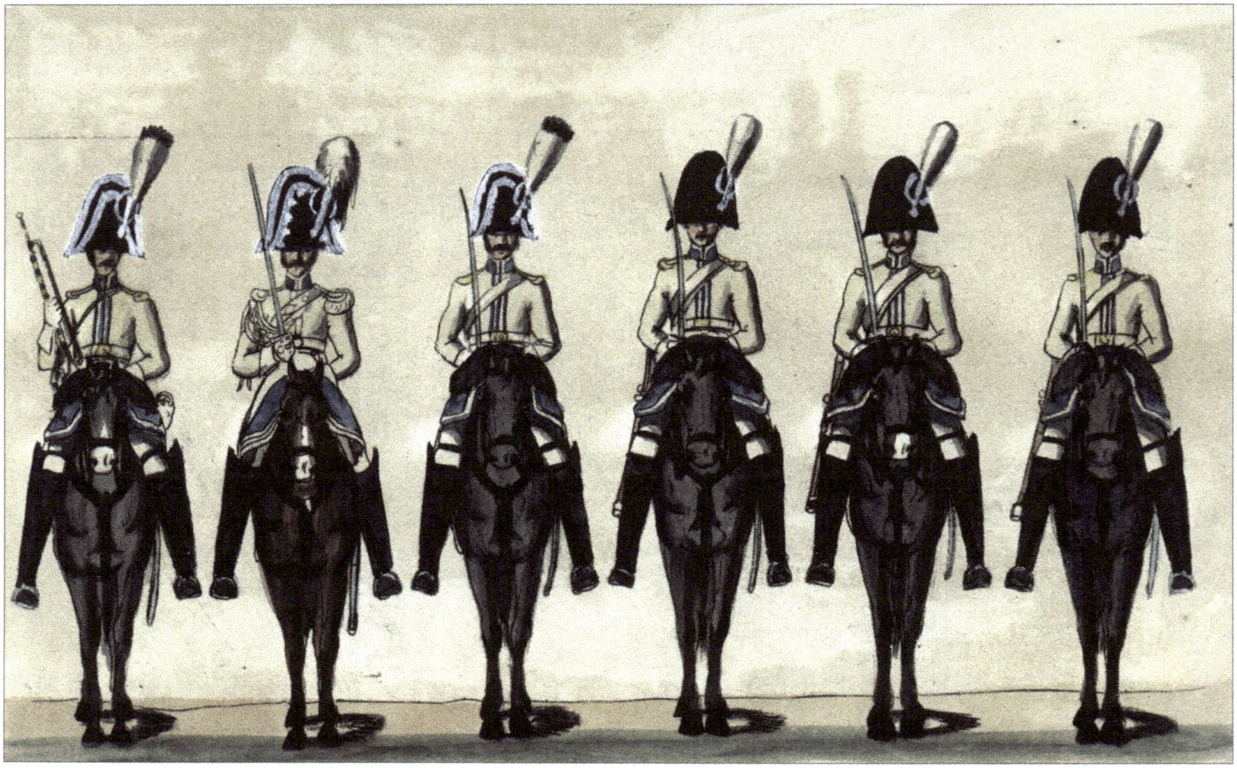

Prussia cuirassiers 1806

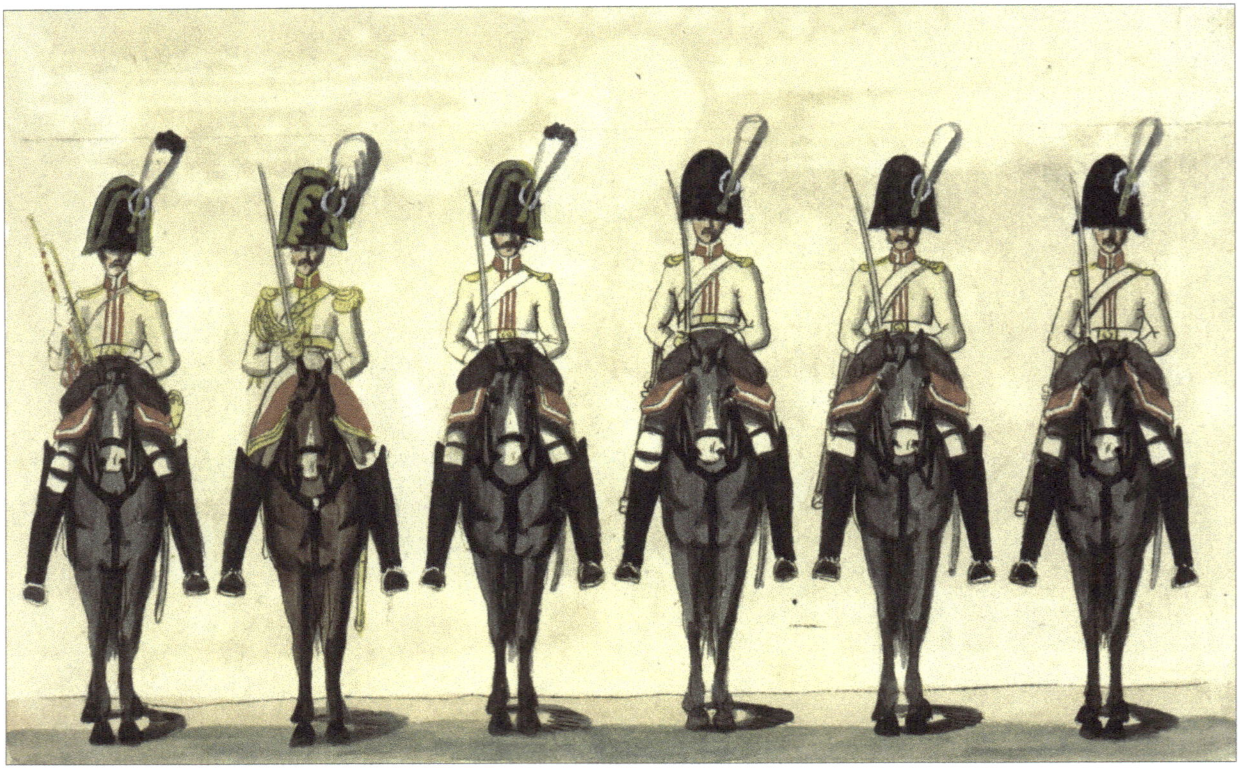

Prussia cuirassiers 1806

# THE PLATES
# OF BAVARIAN ARMY

1806 Bayer infantry of line 1 Leibregiment

1806 Bayer infantry of line 2 Kurprinz

1806 Bayer infantry of line 4 Weichs

1806 Bayer infantry of line 5 Preysing

1806 Bayer infantry of line 6 Herzog Whilelm

1806 Bayer infantry of line 8 Herzog Pius

1806 Bayer infantry of line 10 Junkers

1806 Bayer infantry of line 11 Kinkel

1806 Bayer infantry 1 light

1806 Bayer infantry 2 light

1806 Bayer dragoons regiment

1806 Bayer 3 Light cavalry Kronprinz

1806 Bayer 4 Light cavalry Konig

# THE PLATES
# OF WURTEMBERG,
# WETFALIA, HESSE
# & SAX-WEIMAR ARMIES

1809 Hesse Hussar squadron below Leib grenadier

1809 Westfalia 5th line regiment - voltigeur and grenadier (below)

1809 Westfalia chasseur and carabineers (below) of line regiment

1809 Westfalia grenadier and voltigeurs (below) of line regiment

1809 Westfalia grenadier and chasseurs (below) of Guard regiment

1809 Westfalia Light cavalry of line regiment 1 and 2 (below)

1809 Westfalia Light cavalry of the Guard - 1809 Wurtemberg infantry (below)

1809 Wurtemberg infantry line regiment 1 and 3 (below)

1809 Wurtemberg infantry line regiment 2 grenadier company (below)

1809 Wurtemberg infantry line regiment 6 grenadier company (below)

1809 Wurtemberg line grenadier and Guard grenadier (below)

1813 Wurtemberg grenadier regiment 2 and 3 (below)

1813 Wurtemberg heavy cavalry

1813 Wurtemberg line cavalry

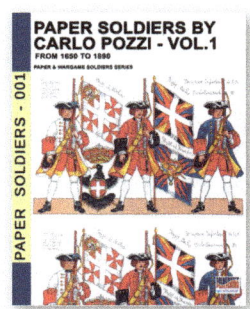

1809 Sax Weimar jager infantry

# PAPER SOLDIERS ALREADY PUBLISHED & IN WORKING

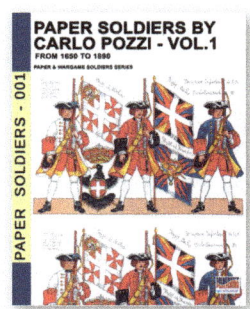
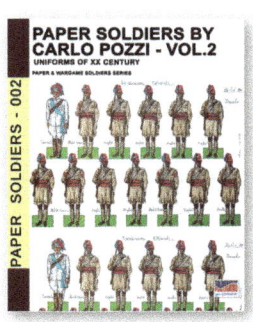
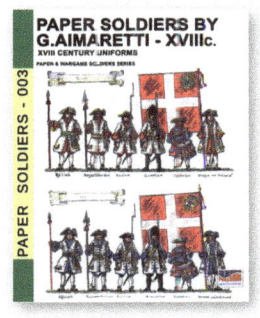
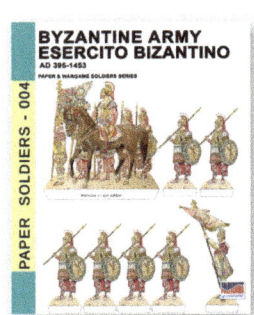
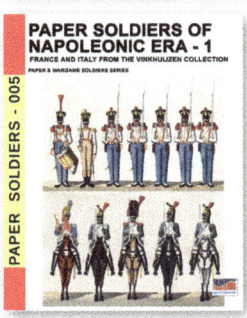
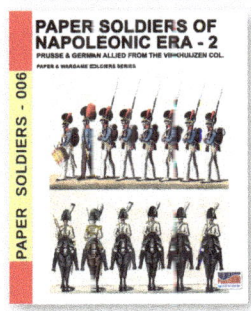

www.ingramcontent.com/pod-product-compliance
Lightning Source LLC
Chambersburg PA
CBHW041155120626
46547CB00020B/3220